MW00914531

BRUSH

A 1950s Lefranc promotional piece for its gouaches is in the shape of a painter's palette.

BRUSH

DANIEL ROZENSZTROCH AND SHIRI SLAVIN

PHOTOGRAPHS: MARC SCHWARTZ

TEXT: LAURENCE SALMON   RESEARCH: STEFANIA DI PETRILLO

DESIGN: STAFFORD CLIFF

POINTED LEAF PRESS, LLC.

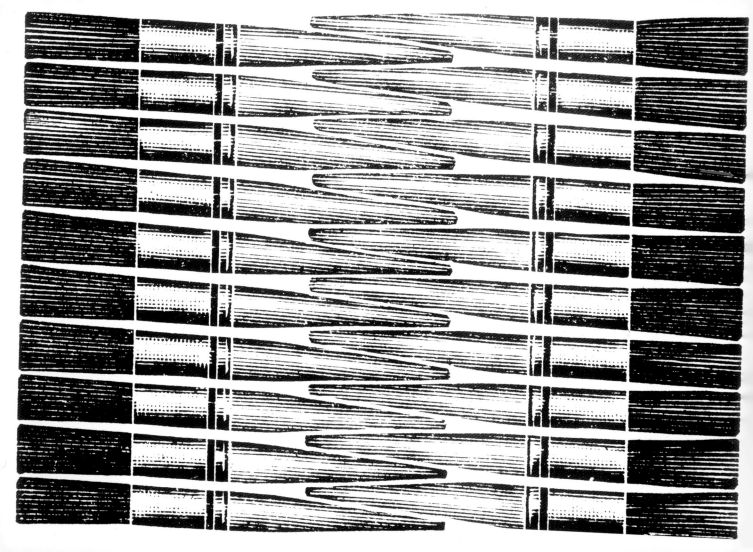

CONTENTS

PREFACE

I see myself more as an observer than a collector. Merely amassing objects doesn't do much for me; rather, I am interested in the stories they tell, in comparing one thing to another, telling them apart, and categorizing them in order to establish a nomenclature, a chronology, a system of classification. I try to assess the diversity of their forms in order to understand how their functions evolved. This is what has motivated each of my "collections."

I have assembled many different collections, and often work on them simultaneously. But they always share one thing in common: my passion for the quotidian—the object that reflects the daily lives of people across time and nationalities; the insignificant, banal object whose purpose is only to serve; those things that are so often thrown away or forgotten, and so rarely preserved.

For many years, this kind of object has consumed my thoughts. Soon after my hanger collection was exhibited, my mind turned to brushes, those ancient household tools that can be found everywhere throughout the world. The story of this collection is a little bit different from the previous ones because it was created by two people. Like me, my friend Shiri Slavin finds beauty in the everyday. Each of us already had the beginnings of a collection, great examples of brushes brought back from our trips to Africa, Asia, and Israel. We decided to explore the subject and supplement our knowledge by working together. When you are working alone, gathering objects can take a long time. This time around, everything went much more quickly. We also both had friends who actively participated in our obsession. Everyone explored every hardware store in their neighborhoods, scoured flea markets, and surfed the Web in search of rare or unusual pieces. This explains the extraordinary quantity of brushes that we have catalogued: close to 2,000 models from every time period and every country. (By comparison, the hanger collection consisted of only 350 specimens.)

These brushes constitute a unique, personal inventory. Our goal, however, was not to be exhaustive. Rather, we wanted to look again at this plain object's sentimental history and its aesthetic tradition.

Alongside the most common of these brushes are treasures of fantasy and invention that at once shock and seduce. It is not often that one has access to such a range of curiosities. And the public success of the hanger collection proved to me that, from Paris to Montreal, an exhibition that focuses on simple domestic objects can be remarkably surprising.

I do not look upon any of these everyday objects with a sense of nostalgia. Instead, they are bearers of a rich heritage replete with information that helps us understand our life today. This sense of history is what I hope to convey and share here.—D.R.

Previous pages left: *An old store in Paris selling household goods, as it looked around 1900.*

Opposite left: *A broom vendor, lithograph by Carle Vernet dates from around 1820.*

Opposite right: *A Chinese street vendor selling brushes, dusters, and kitchen items in the 1960s.*

Right: *In a workshop in the South of France in 1930, brooms were made in the traditional manner—from dried sorghum grass.*

In *The Nature of Things* (1942), French poet Francis Ponge lyrically describes a crate, a candle, and a washing machine. Not once, though, does he depict a scrub brush or a broom, and this is unfortunate. Such a simple household tool should have been of the utmost interest to this poet of the ordinary. The brush is in fact exactly the sort of object Ponge treats in his book: those things we see so much we no longer really see at all. Who doesn't know what a brush is? The commonness of its use leads us to believe that there is little to say about it, that there's nothing to it. Like all such objects, the brush has been unjustly condemned to silence. With just a little probing, however, one might succeed in awakening this talkative witness of our history.

Take the toothbrush, for example. This ordinary object contains invaluable knowledge, not the least of which involves its origins. Invented in China in the 15th century, it was first made out of bamboo or bone with bristles of Siberian boar's hair. In Europe, people for a long time used silk cord, an ancestor of dental floss, for cleaning their teeth, before adopting in the 19th century the silver or copper toothpick. Hygienists before their time, the English would be the first, starting in 1780, to mass-produce tooth-brushes. This is to be credited to William Addis, who invented the toothbrush while in debtor's prison in London. Once he was released, he threw himself into selling his bone and cow-hair toothbrush under the name of "Wisdom Toothbrushes, Limited," and soon after became the official distributor to King George IV. It would not be until 1818 that the French would register a first patent and start manufacturing bone toothbrushes near Paris.

This was about the time when the eminent dentist-surgeon, who championed prevention rather than extraction, replaced the dreaded tooth puller.

Brushes also benefited from the medical advances of the 19th century and from the widespread dissemination of principles of physical hygiene, which were taught in schools from 1882 onward. Water, along with bathing, was finally recognized as beneficial for people's health, after long being considered dangerous. Fortunately, the 19th-century middle class saw the dawn of indoor plumbing, although few were privileged with this convenience; most people went to public bathhouses to wash themselves. The modern bathroom, with running water and a sink, did not appear in homes until the beginning of the 20th century.

New rules of hygiene spawned the proliferation of toiletry accessories, in particular in the area of "fine" brushes. Once the toothbrush appeared, one could also find nailbrushes and body brushes. And then of course there was the hairbrush, which, once powdered wigs had gone out of style, regained grace in the eyes of the upper classes. And at last, the shaving brush, tentatively introduced in 1750, became indispensable for men.

The use of this type of toiletry brush increased with the rise of factories. This was the case in England and then in France, where fine brushes had begun to be made by *tabletiers*—button makers who worked with mother-of-pearl and bone before the process was mechanized by the first machines in 1890. Desperate for work, the *tabletiers* took up brushmaking, which they could do easily enough because the primary materials and tools were the same as those used in their original craft. Photographs from the time show men and their wives working in their homes, making a dozen pieces a day. The handles of the toothbrushes were carved in cow bone, then attached to fine boar's hair bristles with either linen thread or brass wire.

This type of production, of course, had nothing to do with the output generated by brush factories during the industrial age. This shift was reinforced by the introduction of the railroad, which expanded the distribution of merchandise and more advanced materials. These factories relied heavily on the wood from vast local forests, especially beech and chestnut, but not

Opposite left: *A page from the 1899 catalogue for the Sloggatt & Cotter Company store in New York.*

Opposite right: *A page from the 1937 catalogue for the Grand Bazar de l'Hotel de Ville in Paris.*

Brush Department.

HAIR BRUSHES.

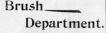

No. 699. 75c doz. Full size 10c Hair Brush, highly polished, light wood, black tampico centre, outside row white tampico, best value ever offered.............................$0.75

No. 711. Same shape, large size, highly polished light wood, oval, grey black tampico center with outside row of white bristles.............................1.00

No. 648. $1.10 doz. Mahogany finish, full size, oval, black tampico bristles with outside row of pure black bristles.............................$1.10

No. 666. $1 35 doz. No. 666. Extra large size Barber Brush, light back with dark grey tampico centre and outside row of white bristles.............................$1.35

No. 382. $1.50 doz. No. 382. Square pattern, natural finish, mahogany back, all white mixed bristles, $1.50

No. 298. $1.75 doz. No. 298. Oval shape, red polished backs, outside row white bristles, centre of black tampico fibre.............................$1.75

No. 226. $1.90 doz. No. 226. Square shape, light satin wood back, white bristles outside.............................$1.90

No. 398. $2.00 doz. No. 398. Oval, polished rosewood back, grey mixed bristles.............................$2.00

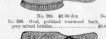

No. 376. $2.25 doz. No. 376. Square, rosewood and olivewood backs, assorted, with white bristles $2.25

No. 68. $2.25 doz. No. 68. Leading 25 cent Brush, light colors, highly polished. All pure white bristles..$2.25

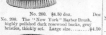

No. 26. $3.00 doz. No. 26. Fine polished rosewood backs, with pure white bristles.............................$3.00

No. 334. $4.25 doz. No. 334. Oval shape, highly polished light satin wood back, pure white stiff Russian bristles.............................$4.25

No. 200. $4.50 doz. No. 200. The "New York" Barber Brush, highly polished dark rosewood backs, gray bristles, thickly set. Large size.............................$4.50

No. 324. $4.50 doz. No. 324. Oval shape, genuine olive wood back, extra polished, full pure white bristles.............................$4.50

No. 808. $6.00 doz. No. 808. Oval shape, highly polished dark rosewood backs, very stiff penetrating white Russian bristles.............................$6.00

WIRE HAIR BRUSHES.

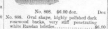

No. 25. 92c doz. No. 25. Wire Hair Brush, polished wood back, nickel bound, rubber face, 9 rows...92

No. 26. Wire Hair Brush, polished wood back, nickel bound, rubber face with 10 rows of wire bristles.............................1.30

No. 27. Large Wire Hair Brushes, with back floral paintings in colors, 10 rows of wire bristles set in rubber face, nickel bound, ½ doz. in box.............................1.90

HAT BRUSHES.

No. 38. $2.00 doz. No. 38. Hat Brushes, mahogany backs, pure white horsehair bristles, curved to brush inside of brim and side of hat.............................$2.00

CLOTH BRUSHES.

Doz

No. 22. Polished light wood block, ribbed, with black tampico centre and white outside, 8½ inches long. ½ doz. in package.
10c Leader.............................75

No. 60. $1.75 doz. No. 60. Heavy walnut oval back, largest size, with alternate rows of black and white bristles.............................$1.75

No. 76. $2.00 doz. No. 76. Oblong oval pattern, mahogany backs, black centre, outside rows white and black tufts of bristles arranged alternately, $2.00

No. 24. $3.75 doz. No. 27. Polished rosewood back with a gold line around the edge, all pure bristles, outside rows white center of black.............................$3.75

SHOE BRUSHES.

Doz

No. 31. 10c Shoe Brushes, light polished back, with handle and dauber. Gray mixed stock. ½ dozen in package.............................79

No. 6. Light polished oval back, with handle and dauber. Black stock with outside rows black bristles. ½ dozen in package.............................$1.15

No. 25. 25c Special. Extra large size Shoe Brush, with handle and dauber, with all black soft bristles. ½ dozen in package.............................2.00

No. 21. $2.00 doz. No. 21. Shoe Polishing Brushes. Oval polished walnut back, 8½ inches long, close rows of black bristles.............................$2.00

SHOE DAUBERS.

No. 7. Plain wood handle Daubers, with black tampico stock. 1 dozen in package..35

No. 2. 10c Dauber. Walnut back with polished sides and end, ½ dozen in box.............................80

No. 3. Iron Handle Daubers, with long polished handle, curved to brush inside of brim and side. 1 dozen in a box.............................45

HOUSE BRUSHES.

The "Handy" House Brush, 4½ inch White Wood Brush with tampico stock and 8 inch handle in package.............................35

No. 1. Counter Brushes. A great bargain for 10c, full length cherry handle with long black tampico stock. 1 dozen in a box.............................87

No. 2. Counter Brushes. Fine cherry handle with extra long wire fastened tampico stock.............................$2.00

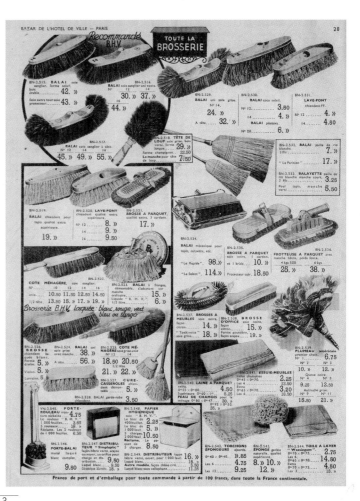

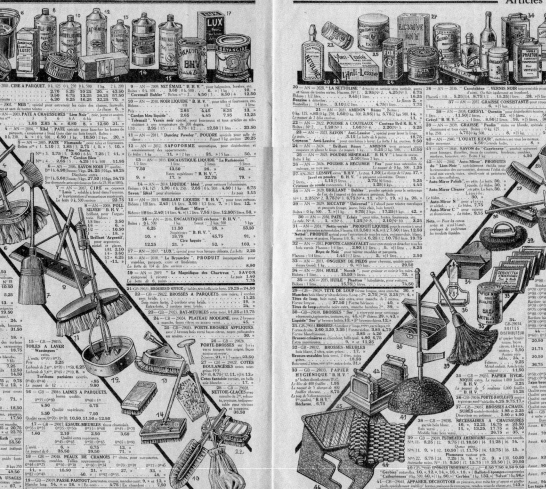

S'il se produit une baisse sur les prix du présent Catalogue, nous en ferons immédiatement profiter notre Clientèle.

S'il se produit une baisse sur les prix du présent Catalogue, nous en ferons immédiatement profiter notre Clientèle.

exclusively. Soon came exotic materials like ebony and Brazilian rosewood, which a refined clientele would value as highly as ivory or tortoiseshell.

The use of these natural resources did not slow the creation of the first synthetic materials. Already in 1890, in Argentina and the United States, bone used in making toothbrushes and nailbrushes was being replaced with early plastics. In 1910, this was replaced with celluloid, which had just been invented, and then with Bakelite. Later came the thermoform plastics, which are widely used today. Around the same time, soft bristles made out of nylon—material invented in 1938 by the American Dupont de Nemours—once and for all replaced the boar's hair traditionally used in China, Russia, and India.

If brushmaking's hour of glory occurred during the 19th century, it nonetheless had its origins much earlier, beginning with the Chinese invention of the paintbrush for calligraphic writing in the 12th century. In France, the brushmaker—*vergetier*—made his first appearance in 1486; *vergettes*

served to brush clothing or to comb the fibers in cloth making. As for the broom, it would be safe to say that it has existed in a rudimentary form since the earliest of times, as a simple stick of wood or a bundle of long animal hair bristles tied tightly to a handle. But the 19th-century middle class made the brush and its cohorts "must-have" items, a fact well demonstrated in manufacturers' catalogues of the day. Getting rid of dust was the obsession of the moment.

There was a touch of the puritan in the bourgeois spirit: a clean, well-ordered house was believed to ensure the strong moral character of its occupants. As a result, household tools flooded into the expert hands of a new army of housekeepers who were charged with carrying out the everyday

Opposite: *Pages from the 1927 catalogue for the Grand Bazar de l'Hôtel de Ville feature large brushes and cleaning tools.*

Right: *An illustrated advertising brochure for the French SOR company, around 1920.*

Dévisser les deux bouchons du réservoir, le remplir liquide **SOR** nᵒ 1 ; la dose à employer est indiquée sur chaque flacon (deux verres à liqueur environ) Retourner ensuite le balai pour faire tomber le trop plein s'il y en avait.

POUR BALAYER

Comme avec un balai ordinaire. Le retourner contre les plinthes et sous les meubles, et pousser devant soi les poussières agglomérées qui ne peuvent plus voler ; aucun danger de taches ni de fuites.

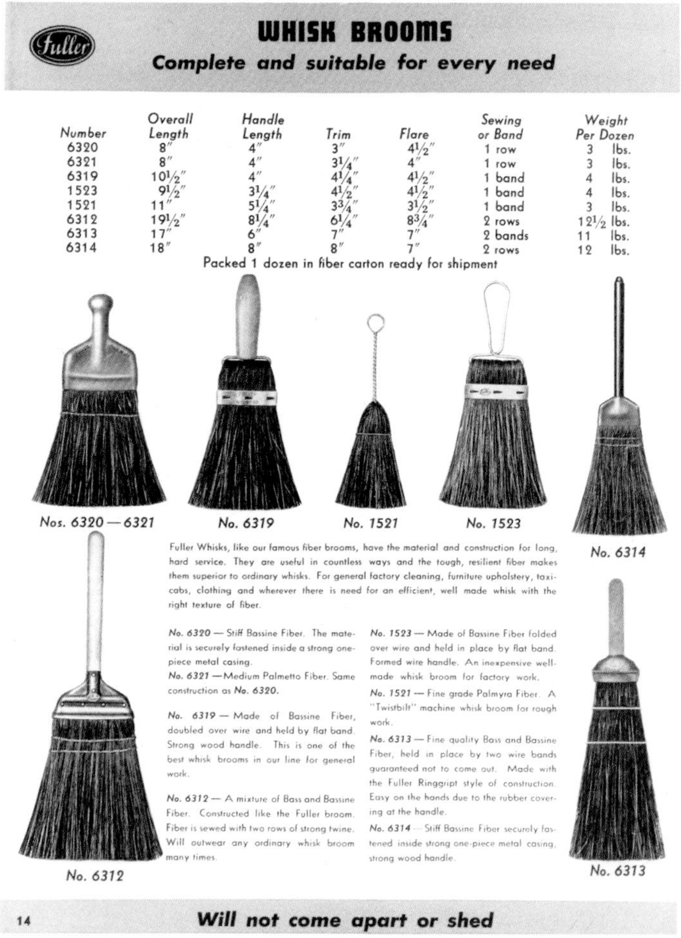

WHISK BROOMS

Complete and suitable for every need

Number	Overall Length	Handle Length	Trim	Flare	Sewing or Band	Weight Per Dozen
6320	8″	4″	3″	4½″	1 row	3 lbs.
6321	8″	4″	3¼″	4″	1 row	3 lbs.
6319	10½″	4″	4¼″	4½″	1 band	4 lbs.
1523	9½″	3¼″	4½″	4½″	1 band	4 lbs.
1521	11″	5¼″	3¾″	3½″	1 band	3 lbs.
6312	19½″	8¼″	6¼″	8¾″	2 rows	12½ lbs.
6313	17″	6″	7″	7″	2 bands	11 lbs.
6314	18″	8″	8″	7″	2 rows	12 lbs.

Packed 1 dozen in fiber carton ready for shipment

Nos. 6320—6321 *No. 6319* *No. 1521* *No. 1523* *No. 6314*

Fuller Whisks, like our famous fiber brooms, have the material and construction for long, hard service. They are useful in countless ways and the tough, resilient fiber makes them superior to ordinary whisks. For general factory cleaning, furniture upholstery, taxicabs, clothing and wherever there is need for an efficient, well made whisk with the right texture of fiber.

No. 6320 — Stiff Bassine Fiber. The material is securely fastened inside a strong one-piece metal casing.

No. 6321 —Medium Palmetto Fiber. Same construction as ***No. 6320.***

No. 6319 — Made of Bassine Fiber, doubled over wire and held by flat band. Strong wood handle. This is one of the best whisk brooms in our line for general work.

No. 6312 — A mixture of Bass and Bassine Fiber. Constructed like the Fuller broom. Fiber is sewed with two rows of strong twine. Will outwear any ordinary whisk broom many times.

No. 1523 — Made of Bassine Fiber folded over wire and held in place by flat band. Formed wire handle. An inexpensive well-made whisk broom for factory work.

No. 1521 — Fine grade Palmyra Fiber. A "Twistbilt" machine whisk broom for rough work.

No. 6313 — Fine quality Bass and Bassine Fiber, held in place by two wire bands guaranteed not to come out. Made with the Fuller Ringgript style of construction. Easy on the hands due to the rubber covering at the handle.

No. 6314 — Stiff Bassine Fiber securely fastened inside strong one-piece metal casing, strong wood handle.

No. 6312 *No. 6313*

14 **Will not come apart or shed**

chores. One also has to imagine how the interior of houses looked during this time: dark mahogany furniture, double-thick walls hung with heavy tapestries, windows draped with muslin, and parquet floors stifled under thick carpets. Houses were dense nests of uncleanliness that required a particular tool for each task: pot scrubbers, brushes for the stove and ovens, spiderweb brushes, brushes for polishing, tapestry brushes, double-headed brooms, and special brooms for sweeping stairs or bookshelves.

Many of these thousand and one brushes had in fact disappeared when the Good Fairy Electricity liberated women from some of their daily tasks. At the turn of the 20th century, Alfred Fuller, an American, recognized the potential of developing durable brushes that were better suited to the cleaning needs of the times. In his sister's New England basement, Fuller was able to design and manufacture such products as a camel hairbrush for cleaning silk hats, a spittoon cleaner, and a long-handled duster specially designed for Victorian furniture. By 1923, just 17 years later, Fuller's annual sales were $15 million, and his sales force had expanded from one to thousands of "Fuller Brush Men," a term coined by the staff of *The Saturday Evening Post*, the influential magazine of the time.

The introduction of electric household appliances put an end to exhausting, all-consuming chores like sweeping and doing laundry by hand. This change can be seen in the phenomenon of the "home trade show," which became an annual event starting in 1923 with the first Salon des Arts Ménagers in Paris. The enormous success of this spectacle of modern comfort—1.5 million visitors in 1953 versus 100,000 in 1923—proved skeptics wrong, like the French newspaper critic who asked in 1930, "What does this have to do with art?" For Jules-Louis Breton, founder of the salon, it was above all about valuing homemaking by providing glimpses of new electric appliances that would soon take the place of other devices. Just after World War II, a unique era of domestication sent many women back to their posts as mistresses of the household, while others decided to work outside the home. No wonder few could resist buying a washing machine to replace the washboard, the bar of Marseille soap, and the scrub brush. Even fewer could pass up two new miraculous inventions, the mechanical broom, invented by the American Melville Bissell in 1876, and the vacuum cleaner, invented by Bissell's colleague, J. Murray Spangler, in 1907.

No matter where technology takes us, however, brushes, those humble tools of the everyday, will always be indispensable. Designers today continue to perfect their forms, no doubt in part to keep them from going extinct. But reinvention is also a way to ruffle our feathers, shake us up a bit, if only so that we once again will need smoothing out—with a perfect brush of course.—L.S.

Opposite: *A page from the famous American Fuller Brush Company's 1946 catalogue.*

Right: *Pages from a catalogue for the English Victory brand.*

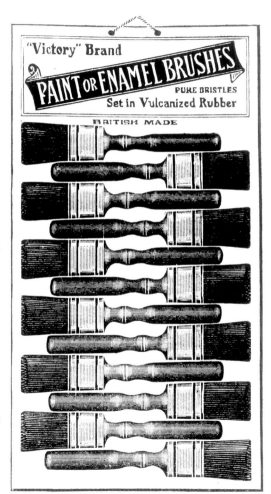

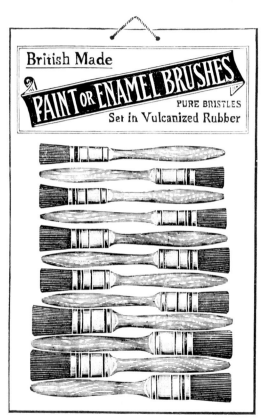

GEO. E. WATSON CO.

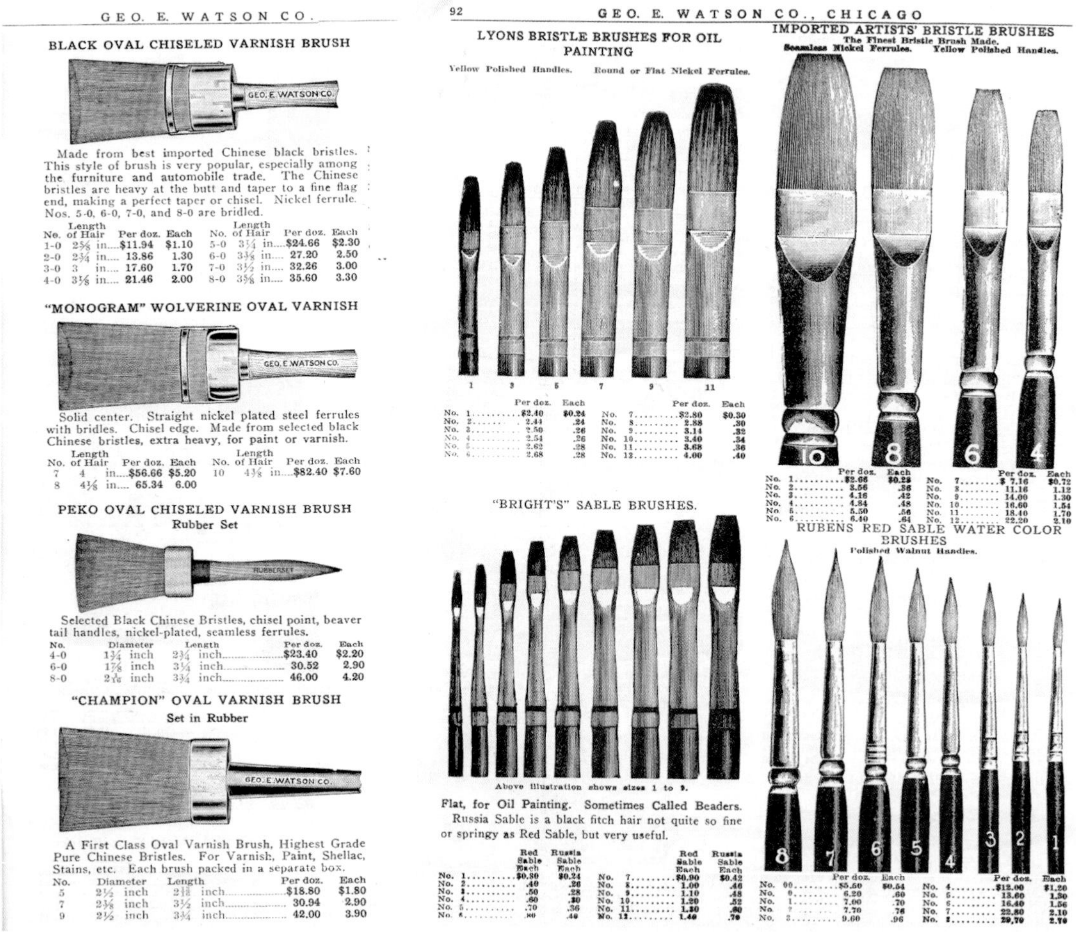

BLACK OVAL CHISELED VARNISH BRUSH

Made from best imported Chinese black bristles. This style of brush is very popular, especially among the furniture and automobile trade. The Chinese bristles are heavy at the butt and taper to a fine flag end, making a perfect taper or chisel. Nickel ferrule. Nos. 5-0, 6-0, 7-0, and 8-0 are bridled.

No.	Length of Hair	Per doz.	Each	No.	Length of Hair	Per doz.	Each
1-0	2⅝ in.	$11.94	$1.10	5-0	3¼ in.	$24.66	$2.30
2-0	2¾ in.	13.86	1.30	6-0	3⅜ in.	27.20	2.50
3-0	3 in.	17.60	1.70	7-0	3½ in.	32.26	3.00
4-0	3⅛ in.	21.46	2.00	8-0	3⅝ in.	35.60	3.30

"MONOGRAM" WOLVERINE OVAL VARNISH

Solid center. Straight nickel plated steel ferrules with bridles. Chisel edge. Made from selected black Chinese bristles, extra heavy, for paint or varnish.

No.	Length of Hair	Per doz.	Each	No.	Length of Hair	Per doz.	Each
7	4 in.	$56.66	$5.20	10	4⅜ in.	$82.40	$7.60
8	4⅛ in.	65.34	6.00				

PEKO OVAL CHISELED VARNISH BRUSH
Rubber Set

Selected Black Chinese Bristles, chisel point, beaver tail handles, nickel-plated, seamless ferrules.

No.	Diameter	Length	Per doz.	Each
4-0	1¼ inch	2¾ inch	$23.40	$2.20
6-0	1⅞ inch	3¼ inch	30.52	2.90
8-0	2⅟₁₆ inch	3¾ inch	46.00	4.20

"CHAMPION" OVAL VARNISH BRUSH
Set in Rubber

A First Class Oval Varnish Brush, Highest Grade Pure Chinese Bristles. For Varnish, Paint, Shellac, Stains, etc. Each brush packed in a separate box.

No.	Diameter	Length	Per doz.	Each
5	2½ inch	2⅞ inch	$18.80	$1.80
7	2⅜ inch	3½ inch	30.94	2.90
9	2½ inch	3¾ inch	42.00	3.90

92 GEO. E. WATSON CO., CHICAGO

LYONS BRISTLE BRUSHES FOR OIL PAINTING

Yellow Polished Handles. Round or Flat Nickel Ferrules.

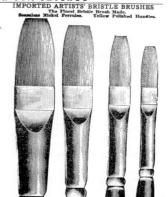

No.	Per doz.	Each	No.	Per doz.	Each
No. 1	$2.40	$0.24	No. 7	$2.80	$0.30
No. 2	2.44	.24	No. 8	2.88	.30
No. 3	2.50	.26	No. 9	3.14	.32
No. 4	2.54	.26	No. 10	3.40	.34
No. 5	2.62	.28	No. 11	3.68	.36
No. 6	2.68	.28	No. 12	4.00	.40

"BRIGHT'S" SABLE BRUSHES.

Above illustration shows sizes 1 to 9.

Flat, for Oil Painting. Sometimes Called Beaders.
Russia Sable is a black fitch hair not quite so fine or springy as Red Sable, but very useful.

No.	Red Sable Each	Russia Sable Each	No.	Red Sable Each	Russia Sable Each
No. 1	$0.30	$0.24	No. 7	$0.90	$0.42
No. 2	.40	.26	No. 8	1.00	.46
No. 3	.50	.28	No. 9	1.10	.48
No. 4	.60	.30	No. 10	1.20	.52
No. 5	.70	.36	No. 11	1.30	.60
No. 6	.80	.40	No. 12	1.40	.70

IMPORTED ARTISTS' BRISTLE BRUSHES
The Finest Bristle Brush Made.
Seamless Nickel Ferrules. Yellow Polished Handles.

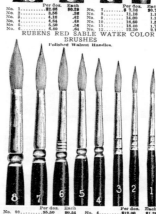

No.	Per doz.	Each	No.	Per doz.	Each
No. 1	$2.66	$0.28	No. 7	$ 7.16	$0.72
No. 2	3.56	.36	No. 8	11.16	1.12
No. 3	4.16	.42	No. 9	14.00	1.30
No. 4	4.84	.48	No. 10	16.60	1.54
No. 5	5.50	.56	No. 11	18.40	1.70
No. 6	6.40	.64	No. 12	22.20	2.10

RUBENS RED SABLE WATER COLOR BRUSHES
Polished Walnut Handles.

No.	Per doz.	Each	No.	Per doz.	Each
No. 00	$5.60	$0.54	No. 4	$12.00	$1.20
No. 0	6.20	.60	No. 5	13.60	1.30
No. 1	7.00	.70	No. 6	16.40	1.56
No. 2	7.70	.76	No. 7	22.80	2.10
No. 3	9.60	.96	No. 8	29.70	2.70

Left: *Pages from a 1924 catalogue showing brushes from the Geo. E. Watson Company in Chicago.*

Opposite left: *A 1947 poster for Aronal toothpaste, signed Donald Brun.*

Opposite right: *Binaca toothpaste as depicted by Herbert Leupin, 1951.*

CHAPTER ONE

UPSTAIRS

When it came to brushes, the bourgeois class wanted what was fashionable. Whether functional or just for show, brushes made for the 19th-century upwardly mobile came in silver, tortoiseshell, ebony, horn, sculpted wood, and ivory. Nothing was too fancy for this materialistic clientele, who were easily smitten by novelty and progress, and so a higher quality of brushmaking was developed.

The traditional type of shaving brush—with soft badger-fur bristles and a varnished or lacquered wood handle—dates from the 1930s to the 1950s, France and Italy.

Unusual barber brushes include a version from the 1930s in its white Bakelite traveling case
and a late-19th-century model in nickel that can be wall mounted.

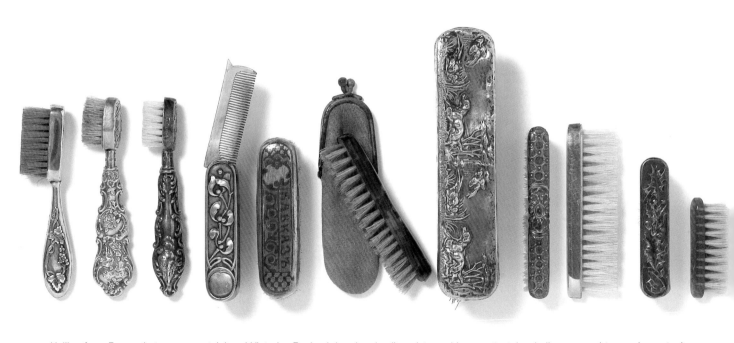

Hailing from France (art nouveau style) and Victorian England, brushes in silverplate and horn or tortoiseshell were used to comb mustaches and sideburns. They were typically carried in a traveling case.

Delicate mustache and manicure brushes from early-20th-century France have ivory handles; at right are two examples in horn for applying makeup.

 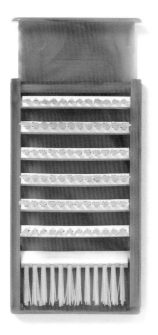  

These brushes collapse to fit inside their cases. One features an unusual art deco design in Bakelite with bristles that extend when pivoted; another in silverplate, far right, dating from the early 20th century, is elegantly engraved.

In the first half of the 20th century, traveling lint brushes from France and England were often wrapped in leather and accessorized with a sewing kit.

The secret of a beautiful head of hair owes a lot to the quality of the brushing, and to the type of brush used.
Shown here are baby brushes in ivory.

These children's hairbrushes, in ivory or horn, are from turn-of-the-century France and England.
Third from left is an unusual design that doubles as a nailbrush.

Lint brushes in horn or ivory from the late 19th and early 20th centuries. The models on the left have curved frames that perfectly match the roundness of the shoulders, while the models on the right are well suited for the flat surfaces of clothing.

Elegant silverplate lint and hat brushes from Victorian England, as well as an art deco example in tortoiseshell.

The toothbrush came into common usage beginning in 1830. These toothbrushes, from turn-of-the-century France, England, and the United States, have bone frames garnished with boar's hair.

Among this other family of bone toothbrushes is a model (fourth from left) from the late 19th and early 20th centuries that has rubber bristles designed to massage the gums.

Dolls also have their own hairbrushes. French miniature versions, in horn, tortoiseshell, varnished wood, or decoupaged, date from the late 19th and early 20th centuries.

Very long lint brushes in horn and varnished wood date from the early 20th century.

A long-line silhouette for these toiletry brushes, in horn and ebony, from the late 19th and early 20th centuries.

Each of these brushes in polished beech has a specific function: washing bottles, dusting radiators, or picking up crumbs. Note the last tiny brush with a tortoiseshell handle, which was used to clean hair combs.

Red lacquer was popular in China in the 1930s; both for a mirror and matching brush set, and for brushes with art deco motifs.

Elegant silverplate frames adorn these lint brushes and long-haired barber brushes that date from the late 19th and early 20th centuries.

This handsome example of a lint brush in colored wood with floral decoration dates from the 18th century.

A second lint brush design from the 18th century is also decorated with a floral motif.

Barbers used these small brushes—in turned wood and horn with long, relatively soft bristles—to brush hair off the neck and clothing.

These barber's brushes, with delicate handles in varnished or stained wood, date from the late 19th and early 20th centuries.

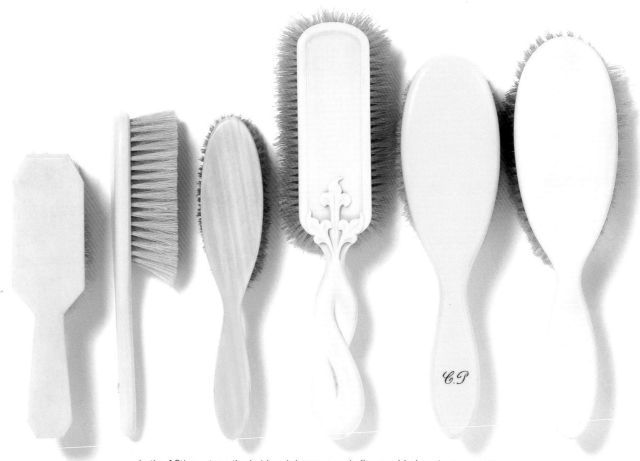

In the 18th century, the hairbrush became an indispensable beauty accessory.
These French models in horn and ivory date from the late 19th century and the 1930s.

Silverplate hairbrushes evoke different styles, from art nouveau to art deco.

These round barber's brushes, with long goat-hair bristles and turned wood and horn handles, date from the late 19th century. The third brush from the left is for a top hat.

At left, late-19th-century English writing-desk brushes, used to dust off the talcum powder that was sprinkled on paper to absorb extra ink. At right, maple burl and birch brushes from late-19th-century Russia were used to dust felt game tables.

English double-headed writing-desk brushes in turned wood with natural silk bristles date from the late 19th century.

These Chinese cloisonné calligraphy brushes are from the late 19th century.

From the late 19th century, a small chimney brush in sculpted wood with dyed-red silk bristles, and a longer broom with black bristles for removing spiderwebs.

These Napoleon III brushes, made of papier-mâché, were used for sweeping up crumbs. Typically, these brushes had matching dustpans.

This crumb brush from Austria, decorated with a floral motif made of tiny glass beads, is from the late 19th century.

CHAPTER TWO

DOWNSTAIRS

This chapter consists mostly of brush designs that have been

forgotten or lost in the past. Now considered archaic, they recall a

world that no longer exists, a world where laundry

was scrubbed by hand, and where chimney

sweeps came by on a regular basis. They evoke

a vanished society in which an army of domestic servants was in

charge of housecleaning. Who would know today what to do with a

wardrobe brush, a spiderweb brush, or a lint brush meant specifically

to clean the master's top hat?

This parade of oval hairbrushes that dates from 1900 to 1950 has stained, painted, or lacquered wood handles.

In natural wood, shapes range (from left) from the half-round "Hollywood" style to the oval baby brush.

Among this series of French lint brushes from the early 20th century is a large rectangular drycleaners' brush with black silk bristles, second from right.

From the left, specially designed household brushes include a broom with straw bristles for cleaning tiles; a parquet brush, whose ends are rounded to avoid damaging moldings and furniture; an atelier brush; and a mid-19th-century street cleaners' broom, made with long plant fibers for cleaning the pavement.

Porcupine-shaped furniture brushes with polished wood handles and black silk bristles date from the second half of the 20th century.

Oven scrubbers with rough bristles are used for cleaning metal, while those with very soft bristles are used for polishing.

Common in the 1930s, these brushes were designed to reach places that are not easily accessible.
The model with black silk bristles, top, was used to clean bookshelves, while the one with light-colored bristles was used to clean the stairs.

In 1910, celluloid appeared as a new synthetic material. These bath brushes, made by the Fuller Brush Company in the 1930s, feature handles made from the new substance.

These pot scrubbers and bottle brushes, with bristles made of straw, sisal, nylon, or cotton string, hail from China, Scandinavia, and France.

Different shapes of scrub brushes are used for cleaning milk bottles, goblets, or knives, third from left.

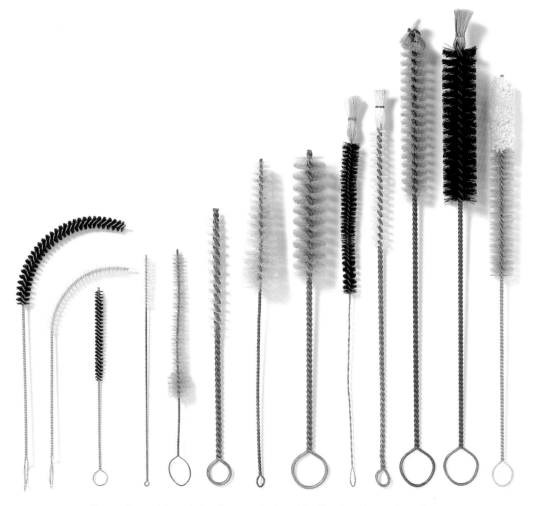

These slim metal scrub brushes are designed for tiny, hard-to-reach spots.

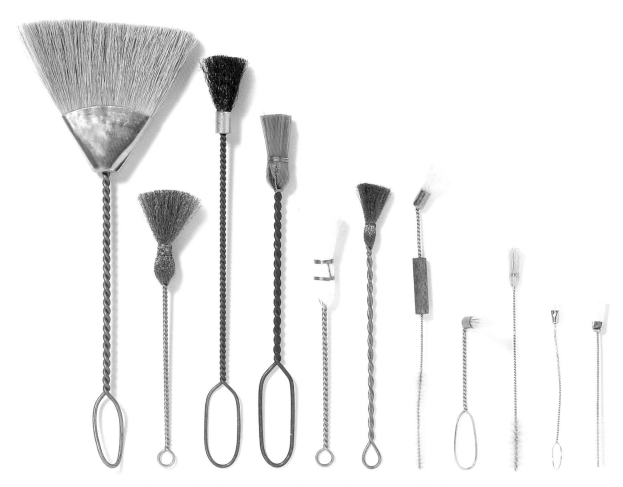

Pastry chefs or laboratory technicians use these brushes with twisted metal stems.

Scrub brushes with particular functions: in the center, a double-head

indrical chimney brush; at bottom, a thin brush used to clean and oil firearms.

Sisal brushes from France and Scandinavia with long angled handles
are used for cleaning toilets or the bottom of sinks.

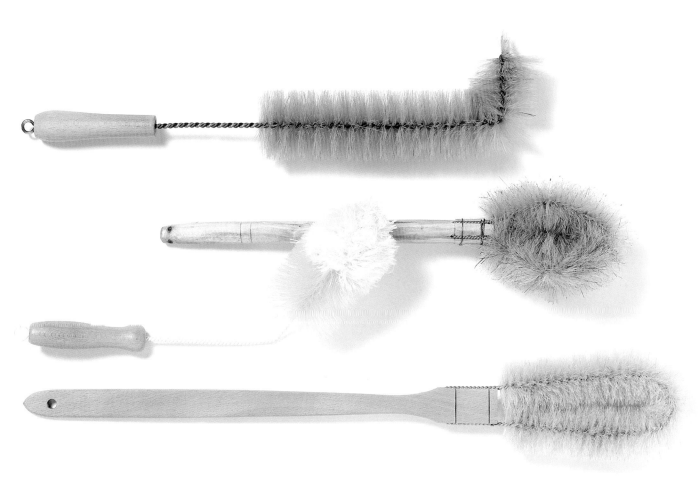

Various designs for carefully washing glass objects are from China, Japan, and France.

Functionally formed brushes: the mushroom-shaped brush, top, could be attached to a long handle to remove cobwebs; the brushes with round heads are for cleaning toilets; and the short-handled brush is perfect for cleaning flowerpots.

Contemporary brushes for pots and sinks are from Asia and Europe.

These different types of barber's brushes, with handles of natural or stained beech, date from the 1930s to the 1950s.

For cleaning shoes: brushes for scraping off mud, applying shoe polish, and shining leather date from the 1930s to the present day.

Small professional brushes for intricate tasks include, at far left, brushes for cleaning combs and other brushes and, at right, a series of brushes for creating stencils.

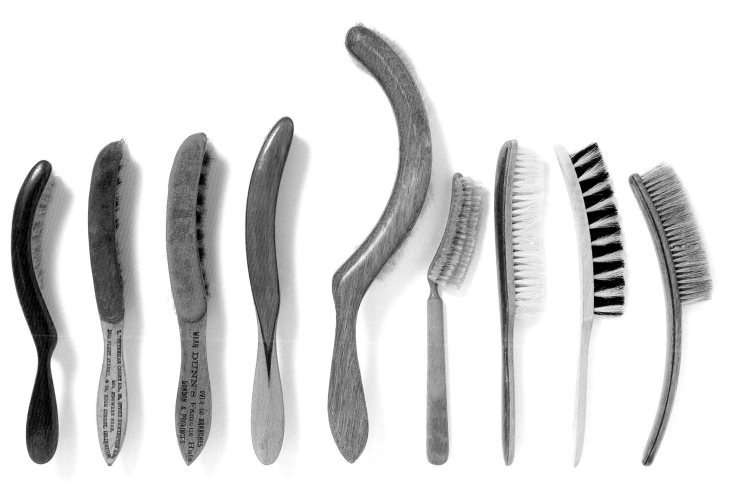

Group of hat brushes from 19th-century France, England, and the United States includes a couple of models that were used as store promotions, second and third from left.

Group of traveling lint brushes dates from the second half of the 20th century.

With wild boar bristles, early-20th-century lint brushes feature arched, straight, or rounded forms.

Everything you need for hanging wallpaper: brushes in red lacquer from the United States, 1950s, as well as a flat-wood wallpaper hanger's brush, with stiff gray bristles, for smoothing the paper onto the wall.

These painters' brushes are made with boar's hair; the flat designs, called fishtails, are for painting ceilings.

Thick round paintbrushes, secured with iron, zinc, or leather bands, are used for cleaning or priming.

Series of kitchen and toilet brushes sport straw bristles that are tied together with wire.

These paintbrushes have natural silk bristles, copper settings, and long, round beech handles.

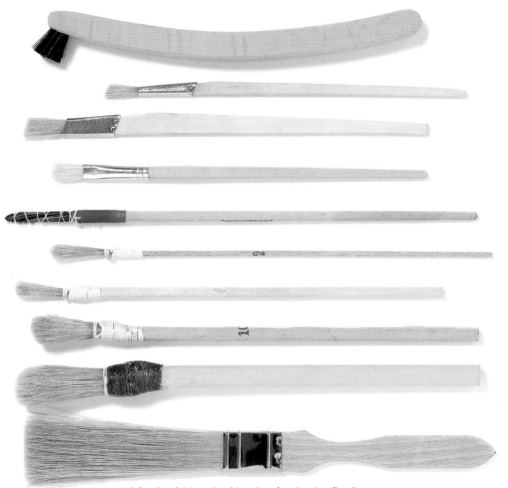

A family of thin artists' brushes for drawing fine lines
includes one very long fishtail brush with white silk bristles for painting stripes, fourth from the top.

Brushes, some used for decorative painting and gilding, others for pastry making, have wild boar's hair bristles.

These brushes include flat fishtail versions for varnishing as well as pastry making.

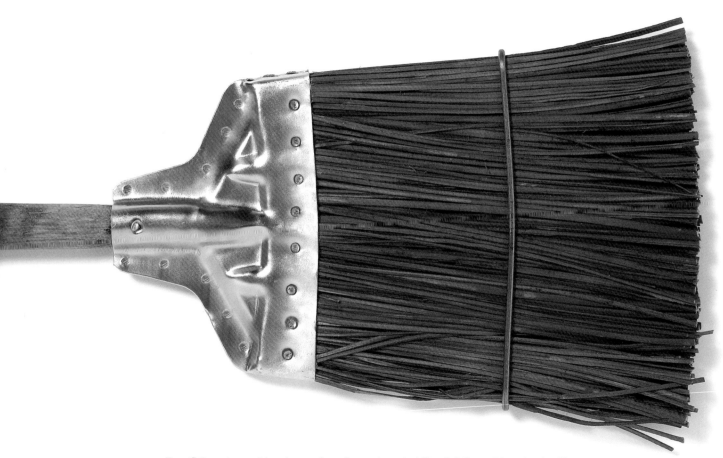

Twentieth-century outdoor broom from France has plant-fiber bristles set in galvanized iron.

Small broom from the 1930s, with plant-fiber bristles, is marked "Fuller Industrial Brushes."

Made with straw or sorghum, these small brooms from the late 19th century to the present were used for sweeping up dust or fireplace cinders into a dustpan.

Made with Indian wheat stalks, these small English and American brooms from the late 19th century are for cleaning upholstered chairs, heavy draperies, or thick carpets.

Different types of small brooms dating from the 1920s include a miniature model and its case marked "Souvenir of New York," far left.

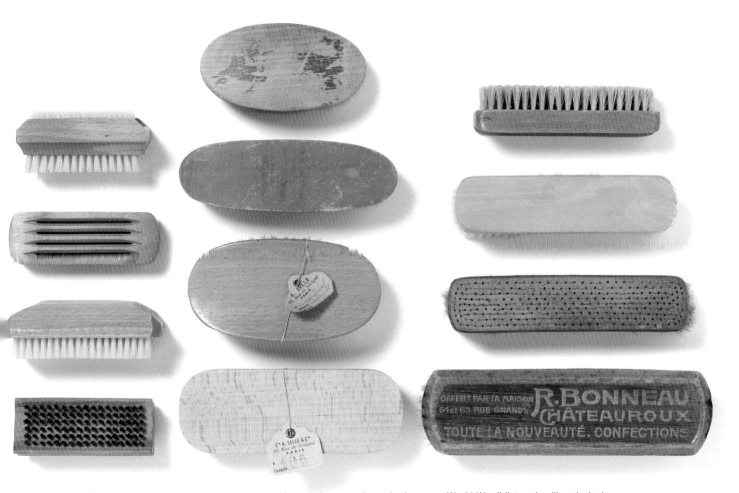

Beech is the wood most commonly used for brushes, as shown in these pre-World War II lint and nailbrush designs. Often, clothing stores would brand a lint brush and offer it to their customers.

Straw-bristled brushes for washing, scrubbing, and scraping are from Asia, France, and England.

Laundry brushes with straw bristles come in "violin," "S," and oval shapes.
The handles are made of beech, which does not corrode even after it is left in water for a long time.

An English curved-back horse-grooming brush with black silk bristles dates from the 19th century.

English oval horse-grooming brushes with monogrammed leather and natural silk bristles are from the 19th century.

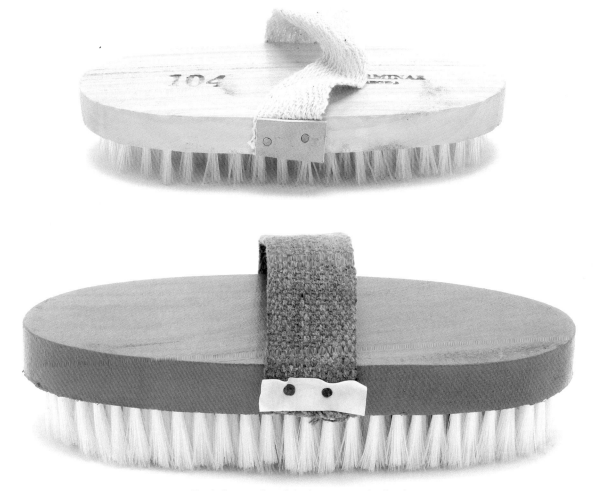

The Indian version of the horse-grooming brush:
oval back in polished wood with a cotton handle for slipping the hand underneath and providing a better grip.

Top: a beech laundry brush with a cutout frame for holding a bar of soap is from early-20th-century France.
Bottom: a round brush for cleaning windows from early-20th-century America has two holes for attaching a long handle.

Embellished with multicolored bristles, clothes brushes from England and the United States date from the early 20th century.

CHAPTER THREE

BAZAAR

This jumble of brushes was found in the souks of Morocco and discovered in the bazaars of India, Israel, Turkey, Mexico, and China. Such mass-market designs are neither valuable nor rare. What makes these inexpensive versions stand out is their bright all-plastic aesthetic, which creates a celebration of color and adds a little fantasy to an otherwise functional object.

A Moroccan ceiling brush is made of two-color nylon fibers that are mounted on a twisted metal frame.

A colorful array of nylon household brushes includes examples from India, China, and Morocco.

Cylindrical brushes with paintbrush-shaped tufts are for washing bottles, pitchers, baby bottles, and flasks in Turkey and Israel.

A family of Israeli brushes with soft cotton bristles are used for washing and drying the long necks of flutes.

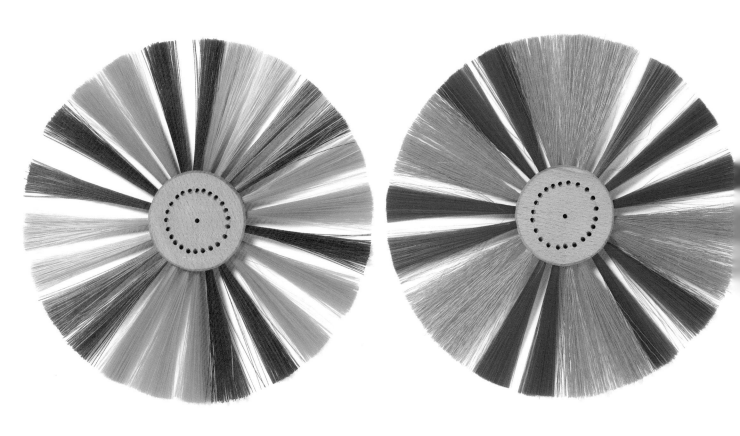

These two-color polishing disks from Israel were made with synthetic fibers.

A colorful assortment of Israeli kitchen brushes with nylon bristles are used for oiling plates and platters.

Mexican plug-shaped brushes with colorful nylon bristles are for dish scrubbing.

An array of plastic hairbrushes from China.

Toothbrushes with plastic handles and nylon bristles are from Portugal.

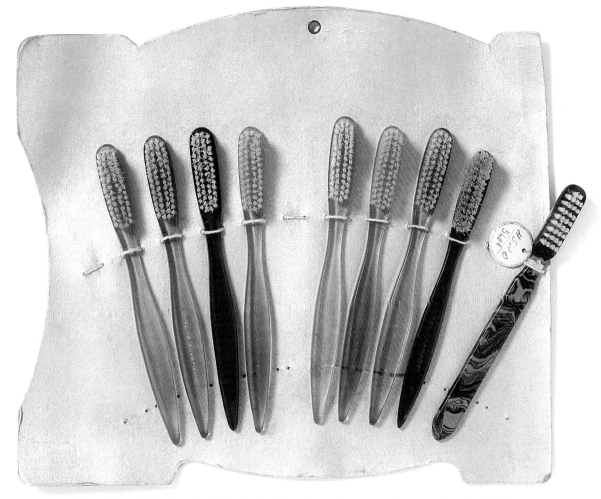

Advertising display of synthetic-handled toothbrushes with nylon bristles dates from the 1950s.

In lacquered wood or plastic, these shaving brushes from France, Italy, and England represent pure fifties style.

Housekeeping brushes from India have long natural wood handles and heads garnished with synthetic blue and green fibers.

Indian toilet brushes in crude wood have colorful nylon bristles.

Two countries, two styles: Portuguese street brooms with durable metal frames garnished with long plant fibe

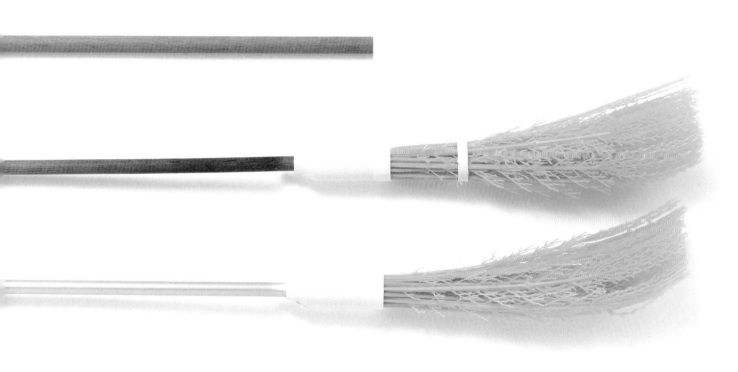

Parisian street brooms with plastic, fluorescent-green bristles that imitate twigs or small branches.

Unusual Chinese household brushes combine molded plastic with straw bristles.

Moroccan brooms have multicolored synthetic bristles mounted on natural beech handles.

Plastic ceiling brushes   and brooms hail from China.

Crumb brushes and their plastic dustpans are from India and Turkey.

A group of brushes from France and China for all dishwashing functions are in plastic with synthetic fiber bristles.

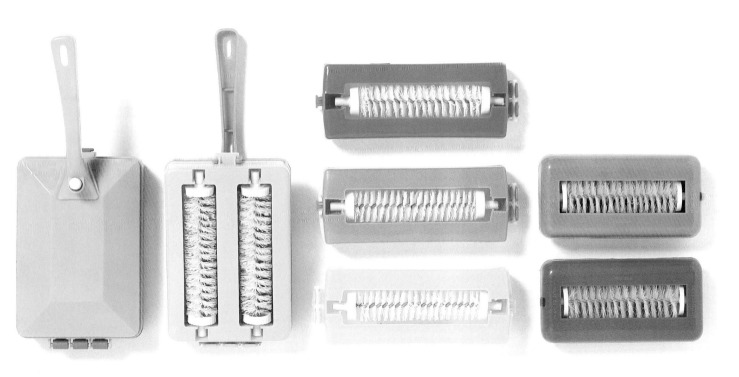

These rotating brushes are used as crumb brushes in India.

These small brooms from Israel and China have nylon or natural bristles and natural wood or plastic handles.

Examples of small brooms with plastic shields are from Turkey, Norway, and China.

A procession of different-sized brooms from Turkey.

Garnished with colorful synthetic bristles, oval brushes from China are meant for cleaning sinks.

Brushes for whitewashing walls, with wooden handles and synthetic bristles, are from Morocco, China, and India.

Dusters with nylon bristles are from India.

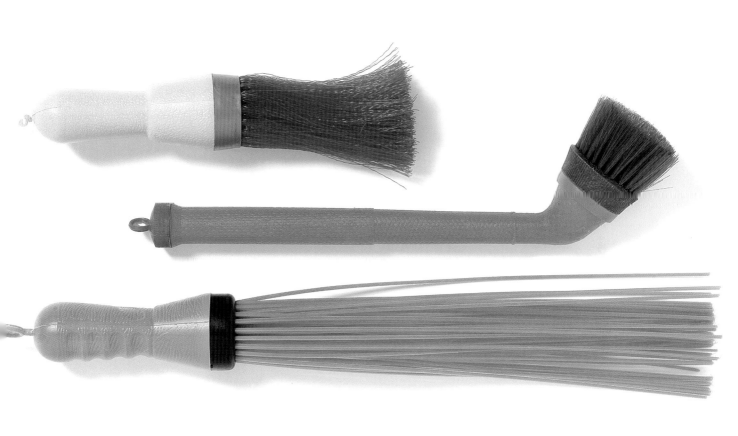

All from India: from top, a barber's brush with long, soft bristles; a curved scrub brush for dishwashing, and a small broom with stiff bristles for cleaning the interiors of cars.

These brushes are used for whitewashing the walls of houses in Greece.

Small brooms from China, for sweeping up crumbs, along with a heavy brush for applying glue or whitewash, far left.

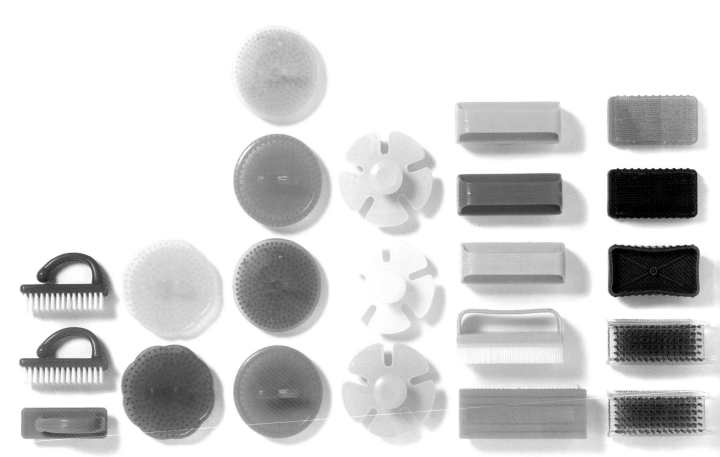

This colorful assortment of plastic nailbrushes, scalp brushes, and hairbrushes is from France, China, and Morocco.

Soft rubber bath brushes from Germany have a nubby surface for massage.

Various types of plastic housekeeping brushes, from India, China, and France.

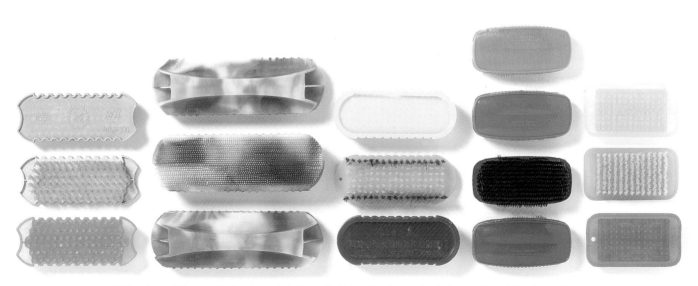

Hailing from China and India, these little household brushes have plastic frames in a rich color palette.

From Italy: a doormat from Fiorucci is composed of 18 scrub brushes.

Chinese brushes with plastic-fiber bristles are for cleaning kitchen utensils without scratching them.

An assembly of brightly colored nylon bristles tufted and mounted in beech frames is from Morocco, India, Guatemala, and Norway.

CHAPTER FOUR

ETHNIC

From Africa and the Far East, these primitive brushes are

the remnants of long-lost tool-making skills. The reliance on plant

fibers like sisal, coco, and bamboo marries the handmade with the

highly sophisticated. The basic, functional aspects of some of these

models recall the origins of brushmaking, when small brooms were

made simply from twigs and small branches.

Small brooms with natural bristles made from exotic plant fibers are from China, Lebanon, Mauritius, and Morocco.
Far right, an American model is made with black horsehair.

Small brooms from Japan, China, Vietnam, and Indonesia are made of coco, sisal, and bamboo fibers and feature sophisticated handles.

Asian brooms made of, from left, horsehair, esparto, sisal, and cane.

From Spain, small brooms made of esparto, a plant traditionally used for paper and natural-fiber objects.

Paintbrushes made of straw and coco fibers are from China, Sri Lanka, Japan, and Indonesia.

Bundles of natural plant fibers were elegantly tied together to form these brushes from China, Japan, Indonesia, and India.

Brushes for scrubbing dishes made with straw, horsehair, or coco fibers tied with string or a metal wire are from Scandinavia, China, and Japan.

Brushes from China and Japan have straw or bamboo bristles, tied together with cotton string or brass wire.

Dusters, along with an elegant goose-feather pastry brush from China, and, at right, a bonsai brush and a bamboo example from Japan for collecting ground ginger.

Small brooms made of natural fibers are typical of Japan, Lebanon (those with colorful wool thread), and China.

Different small broom designs made of palm and straw fibers, from Indonesia, Uzbekistan, India, and Turkey.

Chinese broom made from straw has a bamboo handle
and elaborate tar-coated braiding.

Coco fiber-bristled Chinese brooms have handles that are coated in
plastic, top, wrapped in coco fiber, or made of natural bamboo.

Small brooms from China, Vietnam, India, and Africa with bristles of sorghum grass were for sweeping up crumbs.

Small Chinese brooms with coco fiber bristles are adorned with colorful plastic thread.

These small brushes from Mexico, China, and Japan were used for sweeping up crumbs.

Traditional straw crumb brushes from Vietnam have decorative handles. At far right, an Indian design is made entirely of red plastic.

Different natural plant materials were tied in bundles for these brushes from China and Indonesia.

The more subdued Asian designs at left contrast with two brightly colored Mexican brooms made with tinted sisal.

Made of sorghum fibers, these small brooms with
colorful plastic handles are from China.

Outdoor brooms from Guatemala, with stripped wood handles,
have straw bristles tied with colorful sisal thread.

An outdoor broom from Israel, made from straw, has been elaborately decorated.

Small brooms from Turkey and China are differentiated by their natural fibers and type of handles.

The handles of these witches' brooms from the United States and China are made of crude branches and designed to be hung up.

Brushes can be made of almost anything—from different natural plant fibers, like these from Greece, Turkey, and India, to more eccentric materials, as shown in this Italian design, far right, which is made of electrical wire and has a zinc handle.

These bundles of cane from Senegal are tied and held in place by handles made out of recycled plastic.

Wicker reeds tightly cinched with cotton thread or a metal ring are from Thailand and China.

These small brooms of a cruder style are made with twigs, shrubbery, or roots simply tied together, from China and Barbados.

Palm leaves, reeds, and dried brushwood make small ad hoc brooms from Guatemala, China, and Japan.

Long grass has been gathered in bundles to make these Indonesian models.

Outdoor brooms with long handles from Morocco and China are made from palm fronds or small branches.

This little broom, made out of dried grass, has a sculpted wood handle and is used for sweeping dirt from doorways on the island of Rhodes in Greece.

Designed to whitewash the walls of Moroccan houses, these brushes are made with natural plant fibers, painted iron bands, and wooden handles.

Moroccan toilet brushes are made of stained natural fibers encircled with wire.

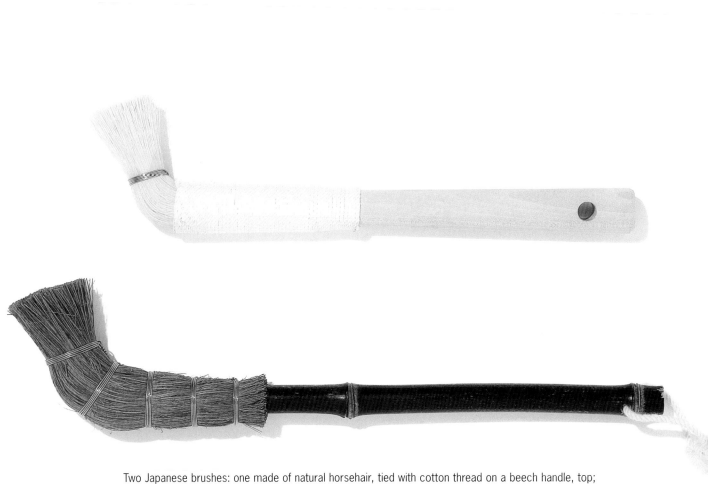

Two Japanese brushes: one made of natural horsehair, tied with cotton thread on a beech handle, top; and one made with coco fibers and brass wire on a bamboo handle.

Paintbrushes with goat's hair bristles and handles of unstripped wood were crafted in Israel.

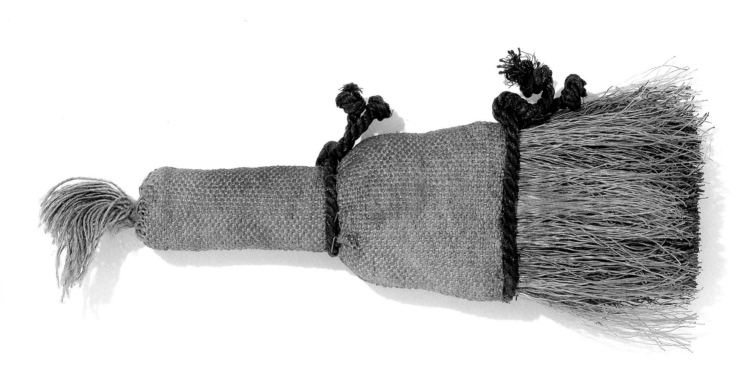

This unique African brush was made with multicolored dyed straw and a burlap handle.

Handmade brushes were made with natural plant fibers and have handles wrapped with strips of cotton.

Three large chimney sweep brushes, above, made of straw and covered in cloth, from early-20th-century China.

Two smaller brushes, one Korean and one Ukrainian, made of horsehair; a carding brush from Kenya made of long bristles tied with a cotton braid; and a calligraphy brush made of horsehair and an engraved handle, from 19th-century China.

Japanese brushes are made with natural silk bristles and bamboo handles.

This series of Chinese calligraphy brushes is made from coco fiber and features braided handles.

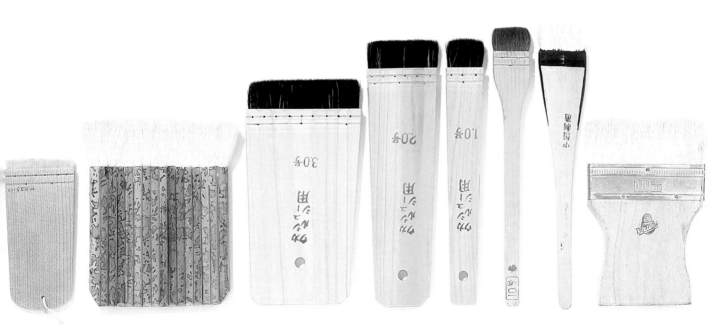

A collection of Japanese calligraphy brushes made with lamb's fleece, raccoon fur, and horsehair.

All kinds of bath brushes for exfoliating or massage, with bristles of varying degrees of stiffness, as well as rough gloves for rubbing made from coco fibers, top left, are from China, Japan, and Sri Lanka.

Bath brushes made of loofah or sisal are from China and Japan.

CHAPTER FIVE

KITSCH

These are objects meant to surprise and delight—

funny, unusual brushes in the shape of a dog, a bear, a

rooster, a hippo, a duck, a butler, and a hoop-skirted

woman—culled from all corners of the globe.

These beautiful specimens of popular culture update

the brush and distract us momentarily from its strictly

utilitarian function.

Character brushes were popular souvenirs in the early 20th century. The plastic rooster, the painted-wood waiter, and the Bakelite cat are from America; the seated man is made of traditional English earthenware; and the carved-wood brown bear hails from Bern, Switzerland.

Folk art objects in lacquered wood and dressed in felt were typical of the 1950s in France and England.
At left, the chef, a more recent model in plastic, comes from China.

A promotional series of brushes, from Avon, with either straw or synthetic bristles, dates from the 1950s.

Japanese porcelain figurines, in pure art deco style, appeared in the early 20th century in different forms—as powder cases, candy boxes, and here as brushes.

Called "Mammy Bells" in the United States, these clothes brushes from the 1930s and 40s have painted-wood heads and bodies lengthened by natural bristles.

In lacquered wood with natural or stained bristles, these amusing American figurines are from the 1930s and 1940s.

From the United States and France, hairbrushes from the 1930s are in blue Bakelite, and from the 1950s in flowered plastic or with a beveled mirror.

Fifties-style American hairbrushes were often backed with decorated plastic, Lucite, or beveled mirror.

Playful plastic miniature brushes are for children and their dolls.

A parade of plastic animal-shaped nailbrushes for toddlers has synthetic bristles.

Made from saddle-stitched leather, French game-table brushes in the shape of a heart, a club, a diamond, and a spade are from the 1950s.

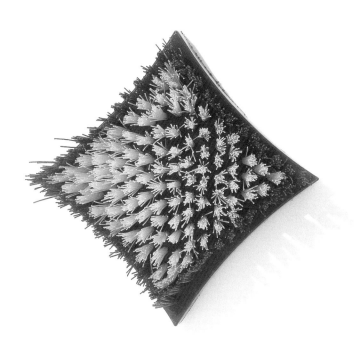

A series of animal-shaped lint or clothes brushes made of varnished or painted wood, from England and France, date from the 1950s and 1960s.

These 1950s and 1960s lint brushes are shaped like a porcupine peeking out of his case, a blue-eyed whale, and a kitten with different-colored eyes.

A European square-muzzled brown bear is the most usual symbol for souvenirs from Bern, Switzerland.
He has been used as a barometer, an ink blotter, and a clothes brush, as seen above in carved wood, dating from the late 19th century.

These charming carved-wood dogs would be brought home by tourists as souvenirs from the Black Forest region of Germany in the early 20th century.

English ceramic handles in the shape of a poodle and a butler make up these clothes brushes from the 1950s.

These fine figurative designs in wood were used for promotional purposes in France and England in the 1930s.

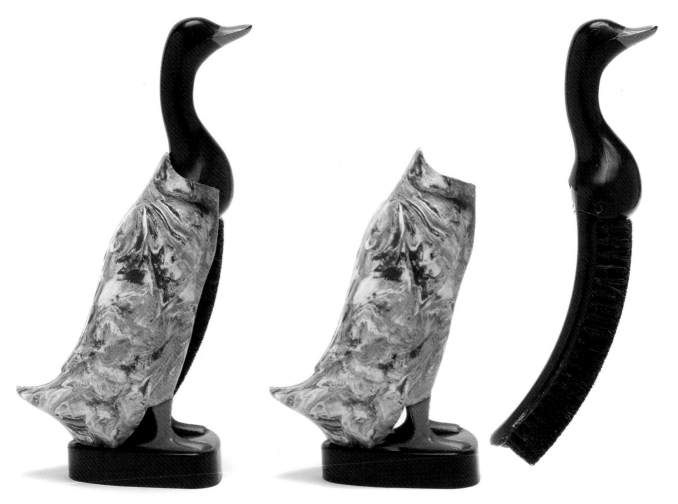

An English lint brush with the head of a duck, and its Bakelite stand, date from the 1930s.

These duck- and parrot-shaped brushes from Taiwan, one including a shoe horn, bottom, are made of painted plastic.

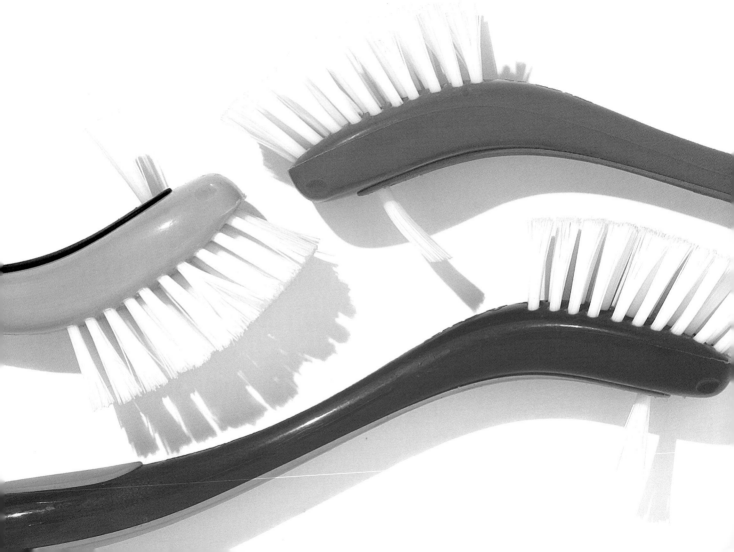

CHAPTER SIX

DESIGN

Design is all around us. It inhabits our daily existence as well as the most ordinary of objects, making them easier to use by injecting style into all of their aspects. The Fluocaril toothbrush, designed by Philippe Starck in 1989, provides a great example. A truly iconic object, it has paved the way for revolutionary new forms in brush design.

From the top: high-tech designs for this double-headed eyelash and eyebrow brush;
its acrylic neighbor; a retractable stainless-steel brush for traveling; and a model with rubber bristles for massaging the gums.

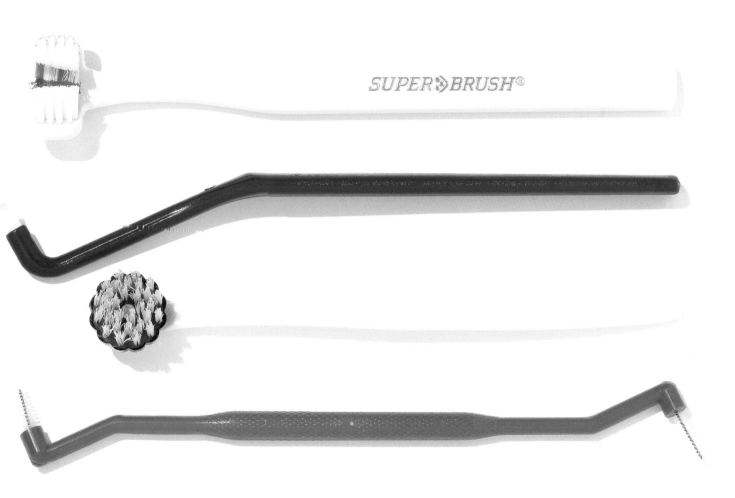

Brushes for cleaning teeth and gums allow for perfect dental hygiene.

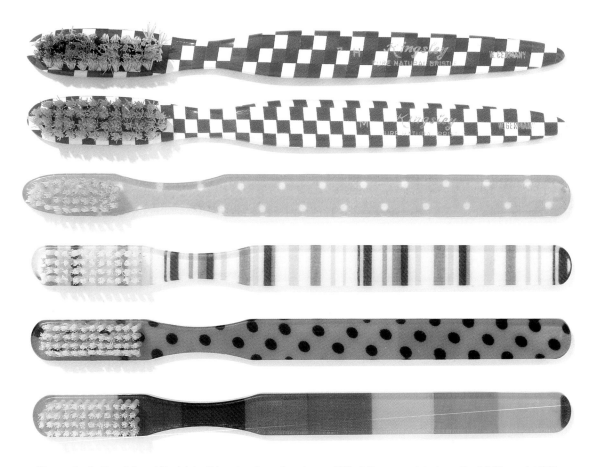

These plastic Pop Art and Op Art toothbrushes from America and West Germany date from the 1960s and 1970s.

American toothbrushes for both children and adults feature ergonomic handles.

The toothbrush redesigned by Philippe Starck for Fluocaril in 1989, with its slender flame-like handle, comes with a cone-shaped holder that recalls an inkstand.

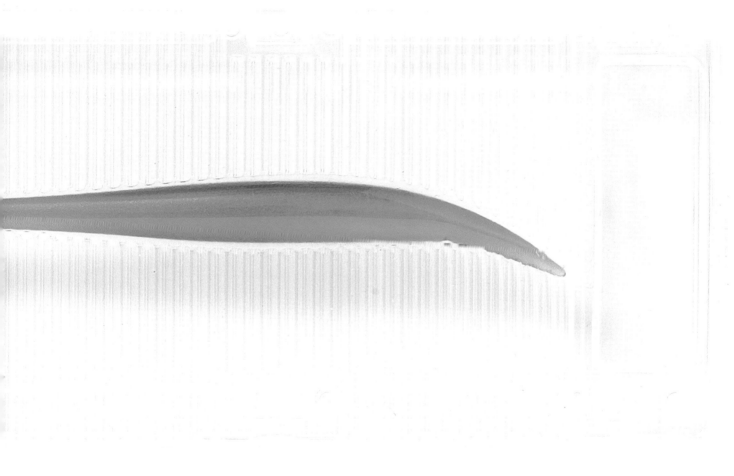

Airline travel kits have toothbrushes that fold up or come with protective cases to allow you to brush your teeth anytime, anywhere.

The latest generation of toothbrushes designed for mass distribution has small heads shaped to fit more comfortably in the mouth.

Nailbrushes and dishwashing brushes prove that good design can be both beautiful and ergonomically correct.

Both body care and housekeeping are served with these contemporary designs.

Functional kitchen brush designs, in stainless steel and black plastic.

High-design dishwashing brushes include a clever model, third from the left, that is equipped with a handle for storing detergent and regulating its flow onto the bristles.

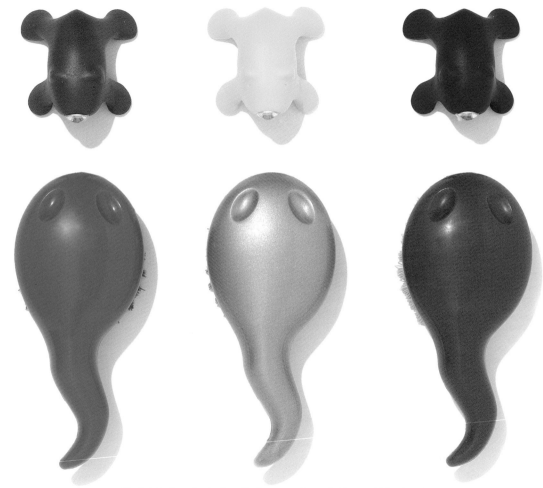

Playful designs for both nail- above, and vegetable-scrubbing brushes.

When brushes no longer take themselves seriously, you can get a scrub brush in the shape of a carrot and a toilet brush, called the "Merdolino," made to look like a plant, by Stefano Giovannoni for Alessi.

The broom revisited: two brooms, one designed by Stefano Giovannoni with colored polypropylene and polyester bristles (by Magis), left, and one with carbon fibers and an extendable aluminum handle for sweeping out-of-doors (by Périgot).

Hairdressers often use brooms that have rubber bristles to sweep hair off the floor. These examples are from Spain.

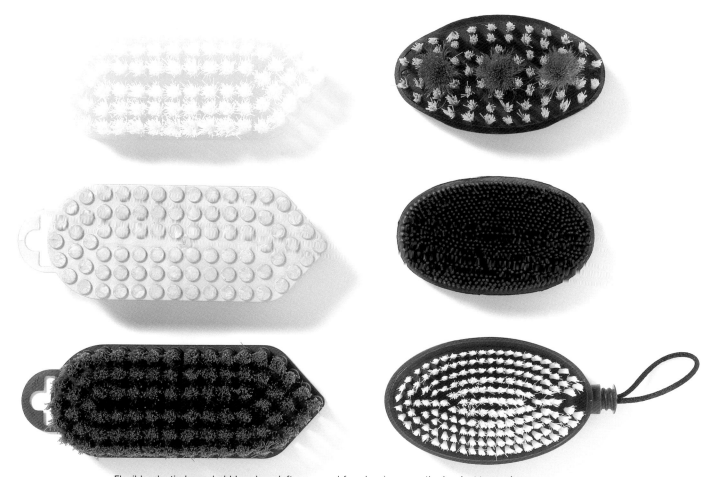

Flexible plastic household brushes, left, are used for cleaning even the hardest-to-reach corners. A series of oval brushes with nylon and rubber bristles, right, also has many uses.

Mats Theselius, who designed these beech shoe-shining brushes for DIM, was one of the designers invited to work at the Institute for the Blind in Berlin, where brushes have been made for the last 120 years.

Among this set of white hygienic tools is an ingenious Japanese design for a retractable broom with an extendable handle, fourth from the left, as well as a beautiful bath brush with a porcelain handle, center, designed by Patricia Urquiola for Bosa Ceramiche.

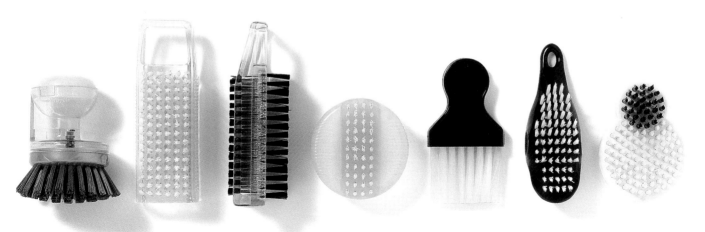

Cleaning and grooming brushes in black and translucent plastic are from Scandinavia, France, and Japan.

243

Designers reinvent objects with intelligence: Carl Auboch made these mustache brushes in two-color horn, far left top; Godefroy de Virieu and Rip Hopkins made the Savon de Marseille soap brush, far left bottom, for Marius Fabre; Konstantin Grcic designed the double brush and shoe polishing set, second from right, for DIM; and Matali Crasset designed the right-angled shoe-shine brush, right, for DIM.

Custom designs for specific uses, including miniature double-headed brushes for cleaning computer keyboards, far left; a left-handed brush by Vogt & Weizenegger for DIM; and a right-angle architect's brush signed by Veronika Becker for DIM, far right.

A small electric Peugeot vacuum cleaner, called the "airbrush," with a round body and a plastic handle and switch, was used in the 1950s for cleaning clothing and upholstery.

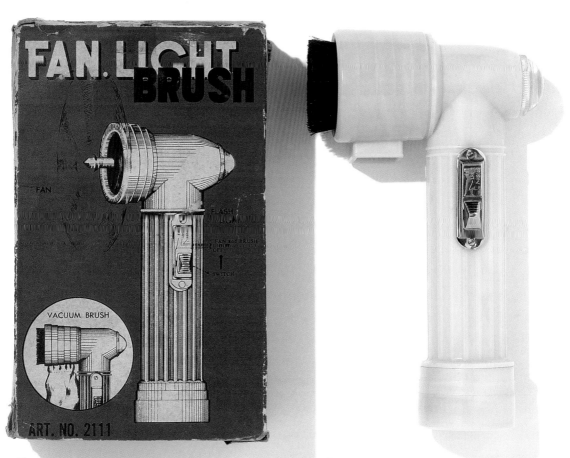

Three in one: a gadget that acts as a fan, a vacuum brush, and a flashlight is from America in the 1950s.

To William Aidan
To Igor Becker, Marit and Shimon Slavin

ACKNOWLEDGMENTS

We would like to especially thank Stefania Di
Petrillo, our loyal assistant, who during the entire
preparation of this book took care of our
cherished brushes, categorized them, identified
them, and analyzed them with an enthusiasm that
never diminished; Laurence Salmon who
transcribed our thoughts with such talent;
designer Stafford Cliff and photographer
Marc Schwartz, who created our beautiful layouts
and Ian Hammond who did the production art-
work. We would also like to thank our publisher,
Pointed Leaf Press, including Suzanne Slesin,
Jane Creech, Anne Hellman, Karen Lehrman, and
Liz Webster. As well as Frédéric Casiot, Claudine
Chevrelle of the Bibliothèque Forney, Jennifer
Dixon and Michael Steinberg. And all of those who
supported us during this adventure.

THE AUTHORS

Daniel Rozensztroch, design consultant and cre-
ative director of Marie Claire Maison, is also the
author of Hangers/Cintres and the co-author with
Suzanne Slesin and Stafford Cliff of the series,
Everyday Things.
Shiri Slavin, a Paris-based stylist is a photo
journalist for the magazine View. She has also
created "Baby Lou," a line of baby products.

© 2005 Pointed Leaf Press, LLC.
© 2005 Daniel Rozensztroch and Shiri Slavin
Library of Congress control number:
2005905351
ISBN: 0-9727661-5-4

*A 1930 poster for the Salon des Arts Ménagers, a
housewares show, is signed Francis Bernard.*

All rights reserved under international copyright conventions. No
part of this book may be reproduced, utilized, or transmitted in
any form or by any means, electronic or mechanical, including
photocopying, recording, or by any information storage and
retrieval system, or otherwise, without permission in writing from
the publisher. Inquiries should be addressed to Pointed Leaf
Press, LLC., 1100 Madison Avenue, New York, NY 10028.
Printed and bound in China.

First edition

10 9 8 7 6 5 4 3 2 1

OUR THANKS TO

Catherine Ardouin
Marion Bayle
Arie Brushes
Anne et Alexandre Becker
François Bernard
Jean-Pascal Billaud
Rebecca Boccara
Amir Borenstein
Patricia Brien
Catherine et Gilles de
Chabaneix
Jean-Charles Chapuis
Tuulikki et
Daniel Chompré
Jean-Luc Colonna
Danouta
Marie-Claude et Magalie
Declozeaux
Françoise Dorget
Saffet Emre Tonguc
Aline et Hubert Fouquet
Jérôme Galland
Faraj Hamadi
Hanamer Brushes
Marie Kalt
Lydia Kamitsis
Charlotte de La Grandière
Mariette Landon
Alain Lardet
Lucy Lefebvre
Marie-Christine Lespinas
Seema Mani
Didier (Service de la
Voirie de Paris)
Sylvia Marius
Valerie Mathieu
Hélène Maury
Marisé Mauverney
Christine Mazelle
Marie-Jeanne et

Jean-Louis Mênard
Dafna de Monbrizon
Marie-Pierre Morel
François Muracciole
Paola Navone
Les Orientales
Christine Puech
Denis Polge
Vincent Quéau
Marianne Rachline
Isabelle Reisinger
Nello Renaud
Gaël Reyre
Maurice Sandiford
Raphael de Séguier
Gil Slavin
David Souffan
Svetlana Termacic
Christian et
Timothée Simenc
Caroline Tiné
Marcienne Toccoli
Ghislaine Tremblin
Reuven Vardi
Olivier Vatimel
Brigitte Verdier
Martine Vincent
Godefroy de Virieu
Claude et Marc Vuillermet
Reuven Wolkov
Dyllia Zannettos

CREDITS

©Boyer/Roger-Viollet, 11.
Collection Bibliothèque
Forney, 9 (both), 15,
16, 248.
HRL-638471
©Harlingue/Roger-Viollet, 8.
©Photothèque des
Musées de la Ville de
Paris. R. Briant, 10.